Afraid Of The Dark

Jo Morgan

© 2023 Jo Morgan

All rights reserved.

No applicable part of this publication may be reproduced, stored in a retrieval system, or transmitted, in any form or by any means, electronic, mechanical, photocopying, or otherwise, without prior written permission from the copyright holder.

ISBN HardCover: 979-8-9897196-4-8
ISBN Ebook: 979-8-9897196-5-5

This Book Belongs To:

_____

_____

Tony tossed and turned all night,

Because of the dark He was scared.

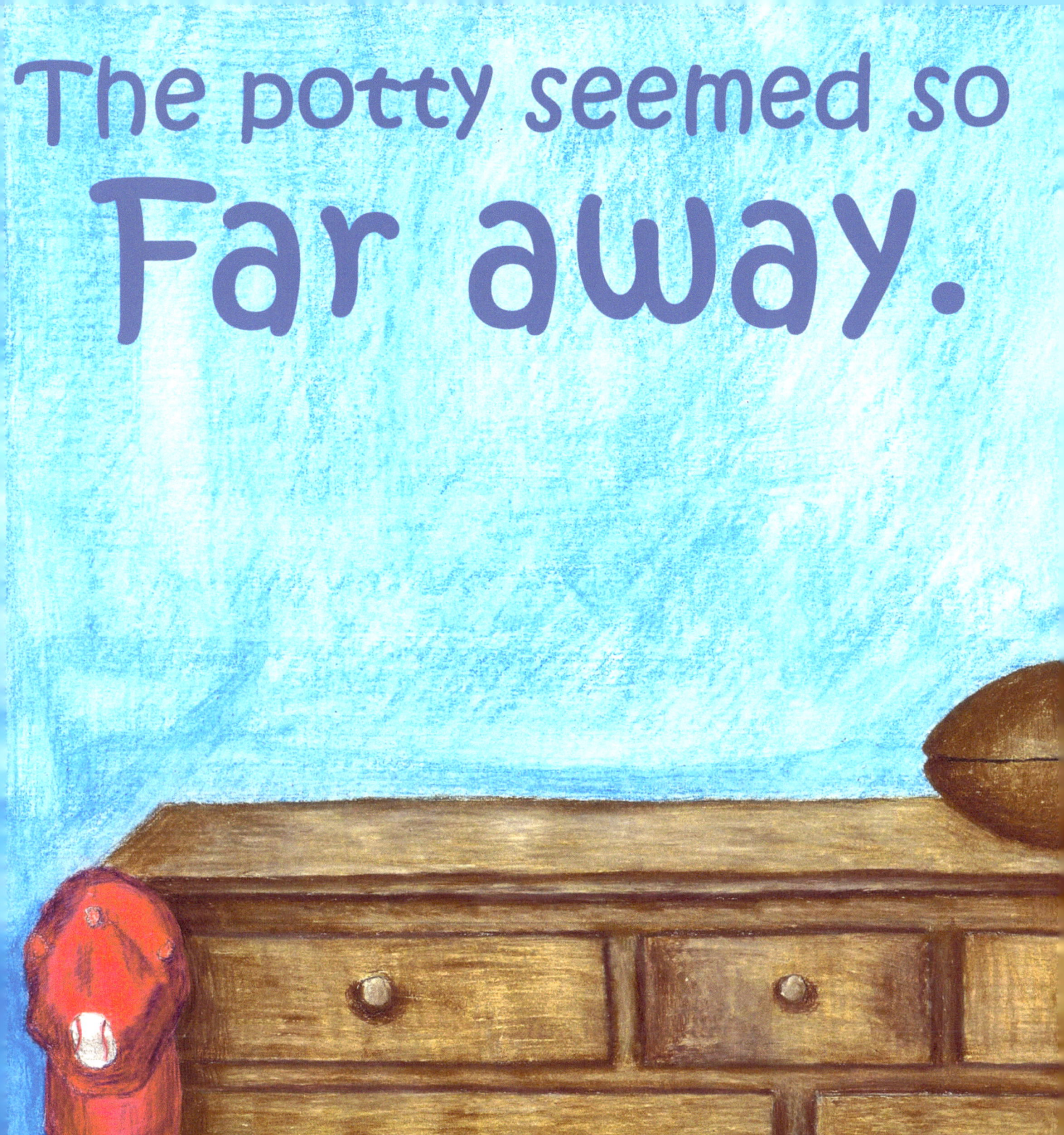

so instead of getting up and facing his fear,

In the bed he stayed.

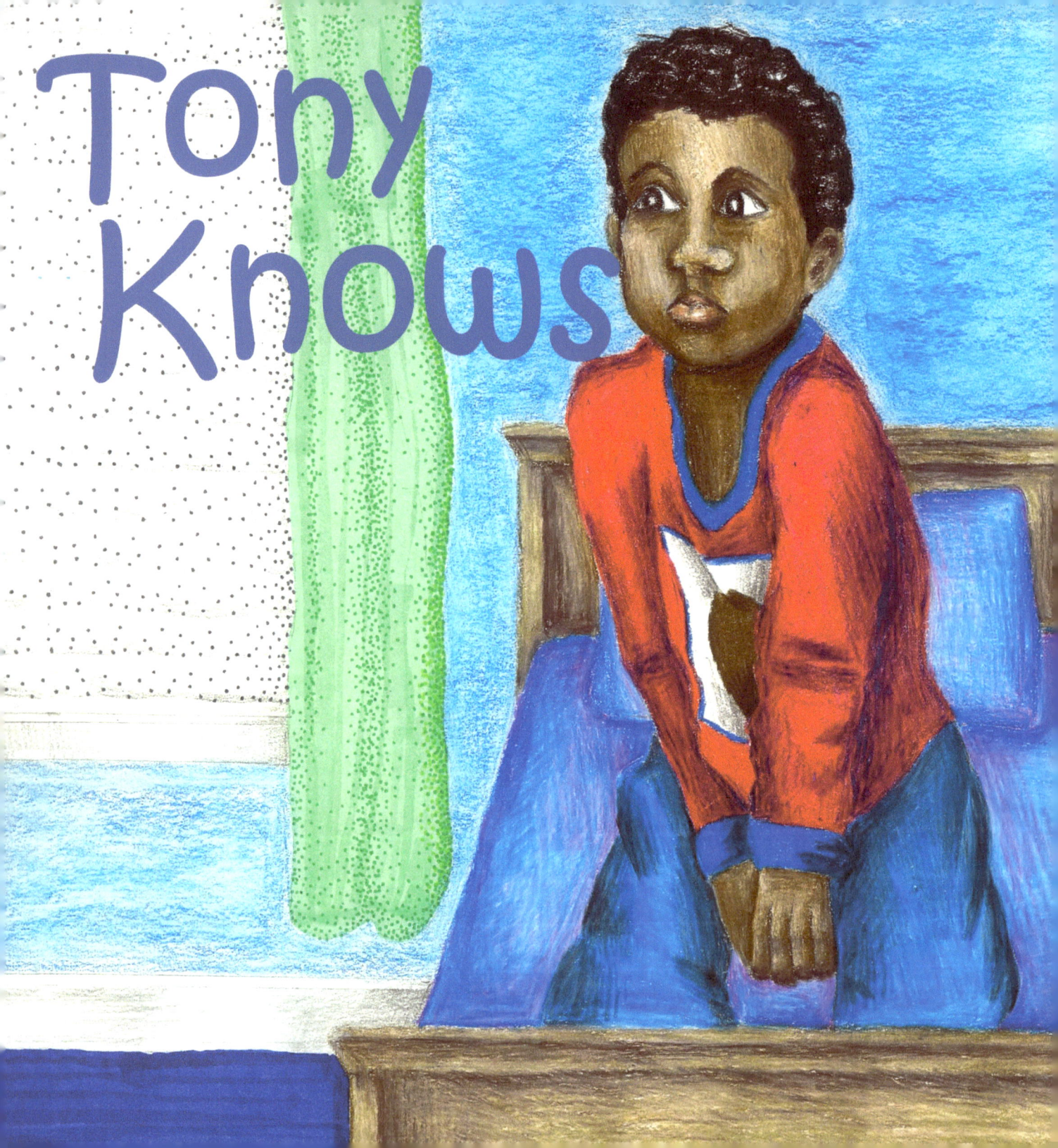

That if he wets himself.

than catching mommy's wrath

And he got up and ran to the door.

out, not because he was scared

but because he couldn't hold his pee anymore.

The end

We hope you enjoyed this story

lets see what you have learned

Quistion:
What did Tony have to do?

Answer:
He had to use the potty

Quistion:
What was stopping him from using the potty?

Answer:
He was afraid of the dark.

Quistion:
What were his choices?

Answer:
Wetting the bed and get in trouble or face his fear of the dark.

Quistion:
What choice did he make?

Answer:
He chose to face his fear of the dark and go to the potty.

Quistion:
What helped him make the choice?

Answer:
Remembering that God is everywhere and that he was not alone

Tony is a five year old African-American boy who is a deep thinker and will usually think of the best way to handle any situation. He relies mostly on the tough lessons through consequences taught to him by his mother and seeking God in all your decisions which is taught to him by his grandmother. Sometimes Tony's obstacles are huge. Huge to a 5 year old, that is. However, he manages to make the right choices...most of the time. You will read about in this book one of the tough choices he has had to make. Afraid of the Dark touches on one of Tony's fears. Tony has to choose to either face his fear of the dark or deal with the punishment he will surely get if he wets himself. Your child will love this story for all its funny moments. You will love this story because it teaches your child about making wise choices.

Jo Morgan/ Author

As a proud mother and grandmother and having two children with autism, I embarked on a heartfelt journey inspired by my children's autism diagnoses. Recognizing the misconceptions people have about this condition, I felt compelled to create books that offer solace to parents navigating the unique challenges, highs, and lows of raising children on the spectrum. My aim is not only to reassure parents that they're not alone but also to let these incredible kids know that their experiences are understood, cherished, and celebrated through my books, I hope to spread awareness, empathy, and the understanding that while a child with autism may have their own set of highs, lows, and everything in between, they are undeniably special and extraordinary in their own right.

www.YoursTrulyJoMorgan.com

www.ingramcontent.com/pod-product-compliance
Lightning Source LLC
LaVergne TN
LVHW070432070526
838199LV00014B/492